GREAT AMERICAN ENTREPRENEURS

Thomas Edison

Inventor and Innovator

Kaitlin Scirri

Cavendish Square
New York

To Dad and Mimi, for your love and support. Thank you.

Published in 2020 by Cavendish Square Publishing, LLC
243 5th Avenue, Suite 136, New York, NY 10016

Copyright © 2020 by Cavendish Square Publishing, LLC

First Edition

Library of Congress Cataloging-in-Publication Data

Names: Scirri, Kaitlin, author.
Title: Thomas Edison : inventor and innovator / Kaitlin Scirri.
Description: First edition. | New York : Cavendish Square, 2020. | Series: Great American entrepreneurs | Includes bibliographical references and index. | Audience: Grades 9-12.
Identifiers: LCCN 2018045339 (print) | LCCN 2018047142 (ebook) | ISBN 9781502645326 (ebook) | ISBN 9781502645319 (library bound) | ISBN 9781502645302 (pbk.)
Subjects: LCSH: Edison, Thomas A. (Thomas Alva), 1847-1931--Juvenile literature. | Inventors-- United States--Biography--Juvenile literature. | Electrical engineers--United States-- Biography--Juvenile literature. | United States--History--1865---Juvenile literature.
Classification: LCC TK140.E3 (ebook) | LCC TK140.E3 S35 2020 (print) | DDC 621.3092 [B] --dc23
LC record available at https://lccn.loc.gov/2018045339

Editorial Director: David McNamara
Editor: Kristen Susienka
Copy Editor: Rebecca Rohan
Associate Art Director: Alan Sliwinski
Designer: Joseph Parenteau
Production Coordinator: Karol Szymczuk
Photo Research: J8 Media

The photographs in this book are used by permission and through the courtesy of: Cover, Stock Montage/ Archive Photos/Getty Images; pp. 4, 6-7, 46, 50, 76, 79, 88 Library of Congress; p. 10 John Trumbull (1756–1843)/File: Declaration of Independence (1819).jpg/Wikimedia Commons/Public Domain; p. 14 Bestbudbrian, Own work/File: Slater Mill, a Spinning Mule.jpg/CCA-SA 3.0 Unported; pp. 21, 61, 92 Everett Historical/Shutterstock.com; p. 26 http://www.mercurians.org/nov2002/images/edison_young2/ File: Young Thomas Edison.jpg/Wikimedia Commons/Public Domain; p. 30 Library of Congress/File: Nancy Elliot, mother of T.A. Edison, LCCN93508597.jpg/Public Domain; p. 35 Science History Images/ Alamy Stock Photo; p. 40 Levin C. Handy (per http://hdl.loc.gov/loc.pnp/cwpbh.04326)/Brady-Handy Photograph Collection (Library of Congress)/File: Edison and phonograph edit2.jpg/Wikimedia Commons/ Public Domain; p. 43 © North Wind Picture Archives; p. 45 akg-images/Newscom; p. 55 A. Burkatovski/ Fine Art Images/Superstock; p. 58 Ron Erwin/All Canada Photos/Superstock; p. 63 History and Art Collection/Alamy Stock Photo; p. 67 Science and Society/Superstock; p. 72-73 Swampyyank, Own work/ File: Menlo Park Laboratory of Thomas Edison, at Greenfield Village, The Henry Ford Museum, Dearborn, Michigan.jpg/Wikimedia Commons/CCA-SA 3.0 Unported; p. 74 Library of Congress/File: Lotos Club, 149 Fifth Avenue, New York City, on a rainy night LCCN2016650281.jpg/Public Domain; p. 83 Joseph Sohm/Shutterstock.com; p. 85 Album/Metropolitan Museum of Art, NY/Newscom; p. 95 Charley Gallay/ WireImage/Getty Images; p. 98 Joseph Sohm/Shutterstock.com; pp 102-103 Aleks Kend/Shutterstock.com.

Printed in the United States of America

CONTENTS

INTRODUCTION

Inventor and Entrepreneur

Thomas Edison was born in America during a time of innovation. Prior to his birth and continuing throughout his life, industrialization swept across the country, bringing machinery and factories. Citizens were becoming activists for movements like abolitionism and temperance and calling for reform. New technology had been introduced that revolutionized communication. It was an exciting time, but also a time of much political and social unrest.

Through hard work and determination, Thomas Edison became one of America's most successful inventors.

An Inquisitive Mind

Edison's curiosity about how things worked started in childhood and stayed with him his whole life. As a boy, he was often found exploring or investigating ships, elevators, trains, and telegraphy. He also discovered a love of reading and science and began performing his own experiments.

When Edison was a teenager, the country erupted in war. Too young to serve, Edison found his first job working on a train selling newspapers with articles about the progress of the Civil War. Newspapers and the telegraph played an important role in the war and would play a primary role in Edison's career as well.

A Scientific Wizard

After the war, Edison worked in several telegraph offices before deciding he wanted to devote himself to inventing full time. Several inventors were working to improve the telegraph and create the next form of communication. Edison was very competitive by nature, and he found himself in many battles with other inventors during his career, including Alexander Graham Bell, George Westinghouse, and Nikola Tesla.

Thomas Edison is seen here in his retirement years sitting by his first famous invention, the phonograph. The phonograph, a device to record and play back the human voice, made Edison a world-famous inventor.

In 1868, Edison secured his first of more than one thousand patents. Unfortunately for Edison, his first invention, an automatic vote counter, was not a success. But he did not dwell on his failures, in either his early or later career. He persisted in his work and set up a laboratory for himself and his staff in Menlo Park, New Jersey.

From his Menlo Park laboratory, Edison produced his most famous inventions. He discovered a way to capture and replay the human voice with his phonograph, created an incandescent lightbulb that brought electric lighting into homes, and invented the first motion-picture camera. Edison established many businesses and companies during his career, including the Edison Electric Light Company, which would later evolve into the General Electric Company. Edison's inventions earned him worldwide fame and the nickname "the Wizard of Menlo Park."

Later Years

Edison's later career included some endeavors that were unsuccessful, such as his iron ore mill and cement business. Despite suffering great financial losses, he did what he had always done and persisted in his work, which included assisting the US government with new inventions that could be beneficial while fighting World War I.

Although he always had a competitive spirit, Edison did enjoy friendships with some fellow inventors later in his life, including carmaker Henry Ford. Edison and Ford maintained a friendship until Edison's death. After losing his first wife, Mary, to illness, Edison remarried and moved with his second wife, Mina, and his children to West Orange, New Jersey. There, he established a new estate and laboratory where he lived out the rest of his life.

Nearly one hundred years after his death, Thomas Edison is still remembered for his inventions that changed the world. His contributions to science and technology have been honored with parks, museums, and awards in his name. The General Electric Company still exists today. Edison's name is most often associated with the invention of the lightbulb, but a great many inventions used today can be traced back to the work of the Wizard of Menlo Park.

CHAPTER ONE

⌒

A New and Innovative Nation

In the early nineteenth century, America was still a new nation, growing in several ways. Although America had won its freedom from Great Britain in 1783 with the signing of the Treaty of Paris, the country found itself fighting many battles over territory as it tried to expand. By the mid-nineteenth century, America's population increased significantly as a wave of immigration headed toward the new world. The nineteenth century was an exciting time for America, filled with successes as well as losses.

The Founding Fathers sign the
Declaration of Independence,
declaring their freedom from
Great Britain.

Growth and Expansion

As leaders of a new nation, the government of America desired to grow and expand the country. One way they achieved this was by purchasing territory that belonged to other countries. In 1803, America doubled in size when it purchased the Louisiana Territory from France. The Louisiana Purchase was one of the US expansions that did not involve drawing battle lines.

In 1812, US president James Madison requested a declaration of war on Great Britain. Great Britain was already at war with France and involved America in the war when they started restricting American trade. The War of 1812 was fought from 1812 to 1815. Many lives were lost, and America suffered great destruction, including the burning of the White House in August 1814 by British soldiers. The war ended with the signing of the Treaty of Ghent in Ghent, Belgium, on December 24, 1814, although fighting continued into early 1815 since word of the treaty signing didn't reach the United States before then. However, neither America nor Great Britain gained anything from the war. They both suffered significant loss of life and great destruction and gained no additional territory.

Hoping to expand westward, America annexed Texas in 1845. However, this led to a dispute with Mexico about the Texas border and how much land America could claim. The Mexican-American War was fought from 1846 to 1848. America emerged victorious and soon added to its western territory with California, New Mexico, and other states.

The Gold Rush

In 1848, gold was discovered in California, and the news quickly spread. In December 1848, US president James Polk confirmed the discovery, and the gold rush began. In 1849, more than one hundred thousand people went west to California in the hopes of finding gold and making a fortune. Some people did find gold and became wealthy, while others left broke and defeated. Still others stayed in California, where they established cities and towns and opened businesses like saloons, stores, and boardinghouses. The gold rush continued in California until the mid-1850s, when the supply of gold had begun to decline.

The Industrial Revolution

The Industrial Revolution in America took place from the late 1700s to the early 1900s. It was a period that consisted of machines replacing manual labor and factories being built to house the machines and workers. The industrialization of America resulted in large economic growth for the country.

Mechanization

Until the Industrial Revolution, Americans had traditionally worked by hand as farmers and artisans. Then, mechanization emerged and changed the way Americans worked. In the late 1700s, the British had learned the advantages of mechanization, harnessing water and steam power to run machines that produced goods much faster than people could. The British had established factories to house multiple machines, but Americans could not use British factories. They had lost access to British manufacturers during the American Revolution. America had to create its own machines and begin its own industrialization, independent from Great Britain.

A key contributor to mechanization in America was a British industrialist named Samuel Slater. Slater had heard that Americans were anxious to create their own machines and hoped that he would be rewarded if he helped them. But Slater was afraid of being caught helping the Americans. He snuck out of Great Britain, leaving his machine plans and information behind. He hoped to be able to recreate them from memory once he got to America. Slater helped Americans create their own machines for cotton spinning and weaving. Thanks to his efforts, the first American factory opened in Rhode Island in the early 1790s. Industrialization in America grew rapidly after that, and by 1815, there were over two hundred American factories.

Early American factories were filled with machines for spinning and weaving cotton. An early spinning machine, called a spinning mule, is pictured here.

Industrialization and Urbanization

When a large amount of mechanization is concentrated in one area, it is called industrialization. Industrialization caused a dramatic shift in the way Americans lived and worked. The high demand for farming and material goods created a need for faster production. The machines that were made to increase productivity required workers to operate them. Many Americans had worked for themselves as farmers and artisans. But the introduction of machines and factories changed things. Farmers and artisans were no longer their own bosses, working for themselves and crafting their own products. Instead, they became one of many workers in a factory line. Workers were easily replaceable because each person had a simple job to do. No longer did one person craft a good from start to finish. Instead, an entire factory of workers each played a role in producing goods.

America's burst of industrialization led to urbanization. Traditionally, many Americans lived spread out in the countryside, often living on their own family farms. But with the introduction of factories, people began moving closer to where they worked. The population increased in small, concentrated areas like cities and towns. Daily life began to revolve around the factories. In some families, every member of the family worked in a factory. It was not uncommon for women and even children to be factory workers. Children were able to fit into small places that adults could not, and the money earned from women and children working was considered a welcome addition to the family income. At that time, there were also no laws preventing children from working.

Revolutionizing Communication

The mid-1800s in America also welcomed a new means of communication. In 1835, Samuel Morse invented a communications system in which dots and dashes were used in place of numbers and letters. He called his system the Morse Code. In 1837, Morse received a patent for an electromagnetic telegraph. A patent is a document that provides protection over an invention. No one else can create or use it without the inventor's permission.

A telegraph was a form of messaging that used electric signals to send messages across long distances. In 1843, the US government granted permission to Morse to build a telegraph system between Washington, DC, and Baltimore, Maryland. On May 24, 1844, the first telegraph message was transmitted: "What hath God wrought!"[1] Before the telegraph, messages were usually sent as handwritten letters delivered by a messenger. Depending upon how far the letter had to travel, it could take several days for a message to be delivered. Morse's electric telegraph could send and receive messages in only a few minutes. The telegraph dramatically improved communication in the nineteenth century and remained the dominant form of communication in America well into the twentieth century.

Immigration

The rise of factories and industrialization contributed to a large wave of immigration in America in the nineteenth century. Immigration occurs when people leave their own countries to move to a different country. In the nineteenth century, many European immigrants were leaving their home countries to

An early example of a steam-powered train is pictured here in the mid-1800s. The steam-powered train became so successful that it ultimately bested canal and river travel in the United States.

first Transcontinental Railroad. The Transcontinental Railroad would be the first railroad to connect the Atlantic and Pacific coasts. It was completed on May 10, 1869.

The railroad became a profitable industry, creating fortunes for entrepreneurs such as Cornelius Vanderbilt and Andrew Carnegie. Vanderbilt owned several railroad lines during his lifetime, making him a railroad magnate, or a person of extreme wealth and influence. Andrew Carnegie invested in sleeper cars for passenger trains and steel for railroads. The arrival of automobiles and flight eventually phased out the railroad, but it remained the dominant means of transportation in America until the early twentieth century.

the country, such as women's rights and slaves' rights. Other movements called for reforming education and forbidding the production and sale of alcohol.

Women's Suffrage

One movement that grew out of the Age of Reform was the women's suffrage movement. This was the push for women's right to vote, and it was part of a larger women's rights movement. During the nineteenth century, there were certain expectations of what a woman's role should be. Women were expected to be wives and mothers and tend to the household. There were many who thought that women should not vote, get involved in political matters, or even speak in public.

Two women who emerged during this time as strong fighters for women's rights were Elizabeth Cady Stanton and Lucretia Mott. In 1848, Stanton and Mott organized a meeting called the Seneca Falls Convention in Seneca Falls, New York, where they introduced a document called the Declaration of Sentiments. Tired of being oppressed by a society in which men dominated women, Stanton and Mott listed the ways that women were being oppressed and called for reform. Stanton and Mott took inspiration from the Declaration of Independence, which declared all men to be created equal. They wrote their own Declaration of Sentiments to state, "We hold these truths to be self-evident: that all men and women are created equal."[2] The women's rights movement grew, attracting both women and men to the cause.

Another important figure to emerge during the women's rights movement was Susan B. Anthony. Anthony fought for women's rights and slaves' freedom. A member of the American Anti-Slavery Society, Anthony was very outspoken about her causes. She supported equal rights for all American

Elizabeth Cady Stanton, pictured here around 1890, emerged as an important leader in the women's rights movement and drafted the Declaration of Sentiments alongside Lucretia Mott.

citizens, including men, women, and slaves. Anthony's views were not very popular, and many people did not like to see a woman being so outspoken. As a result of her efforts, Anthony received threats of violence from those wanting to silence her. Nevertheless, she persisted and spent the rest of her life fighting for equality for all Americans. The efforts of Anthony and many other supporters eventually led to the passing of the Nineteenth Amendment to the US Constitution on June 4, 1919. The amendment gave women the right to vote, stating, "The right of citizens of the United States to vote shall not be denied or abridged by the United States or by any State on account of sex."[3]

Abolitionism

Another movement during the Age of Reform was the abolitionist movement. Abolitionists were people who wanted to abolish, or permanently end, slavery. By the mid-nineteenth century, slavery had become a widely debated issue in America. It was dominant in the southern United States, and many slaves escaped to the North to gain their freedom. Some slaves also told their stories, which often consisted of abuse and neglect. Abolitionists felt that slaves were being denied their rights under the United States Constitution. But slave owners argued that slaves had no rights under the Constitution. Slaves were considered property, not people. This is what the abolitionists were fighting to change. They wanted slavery to end, or at the very least, for slaves to receive better treatment.

Abolitionists were not only white Americans living in the North, but also African Americans, many of whom were former slaves themselves. One man to escape slavery and become an abolitionist was Frederick Douglass. Douglass had been a slave in the South and had escaped to Massachusetts. Once settled in the North, he joined the antislavery movement and began speaking at meetings of the Massachusetts Anti-Slavery Society. While most slaves were not allowed to learn to read or write, Douglass had been permitted to do both. His literacy set him apart from other slaves and former slaves by breaking the stereotype, or generalization, that slaves were unintelligent and incapable of learning. In 1845, Douglass published his autobiography, *Narrative of the Life of Frederick Douglass.* Slavery was officially ended with the Thirteenth Amendment in 1865, which stated, "Neither slavery nor involuntary servitude, except as a punishment for crime whereof the party shall have been duly convicted, shall exist within the United States, or any place subject to their jurisdiction."[4] Douglass continued to fight for equality until his death in 1895.

Education Reform

Not many children attended school in the mid-1800s, particularly children in the South or out west. Children in the northern United States who attended school did so for about two or three months out of the year and usually left by the age of ten. School was not a requirement, and many children stopped attending once they had learned basic literacy and math skills. Schools during this time period were not free. They charged fees for children to receive an education. Children stopped attending school usually because they had to work to help support their families or because they could not afford to attend any longer. This all changed with the common school movement.

The common school movement is largely attributed to two educational reformers, Horace Mann from Massachusetts and Henry Barnard from Connecticut. The two men had a strong belief in public education. The common school movement argued that the government should provide free, tax-supported schools. Attendance should be made mandatory, meaning all children had to attend. Children should not be denied school attendance because of religion, ethnic background, or social status. Simply put, education should be for everyone, not just those who could afford to send their children to school.

In 1837, Mann wrote a law in Massachusetts that created the first state school board, or a group of people who were in charge of education for the state. Mann became the secretary for the Massachusetts state school board and began spreading his message about public education across the country. By the 1850s, all states in the north and west provided free elementary schools for children as well as training for teachers. Some states went beyond elementary school and began providing public high schools and colleges as well.

Temperance Movement

Considered by many the most successful movement during the Age of Reform, the temperance movement focused on decreasing alcohol consumption in the United States. Temperance means to control one's drinking habits. Drinking alcohol had become a normal routine for many citizens. Drink breaks during work were common, as was the practice of gathering at the tavern after work. While some women drank at home, men consumed the most alcohol.

The temperance movement gained a national following in 1826 with the foundation of the American Temperance Union. The group's goal was to get citizens to stop drinking alcohol. After several years, the temperance movement shifted its focus from lessening the consumption of alcohol to prohibiting, or banning, it altogether. In 1851, Maine became the first state to successfully prohibit the making and selling of alcoholic beverages. Over the next few years, several other states followed. These new prohibition laws dramatically decreased the national consumption of alcohol, and the temperance movement was considered a success.

CHAPTER TWO

The Wizard of Menlo Park

Thomas Edison was born during an exciting time in America. The country was experiencing a surge of political activity and social movements. The electric telegraph and Morse Code had recently been invented, ushering in a new age of technology. America produced many inventors during the nineteenth and twentieth centuries, but Edison was perhaps the most famous.

Early Life and Family

Thomas Alva Edison was born on February 11, 1847, in Milan, Ohio. He was named Thomas after his father's

Edison, seen here as a boy, was always curious and eager to learn, leading to his career as an inventor.

brother and Alva after Captain Alva Bradley, a close friend of his father. Edison was the fifth child of Samuel Edison Jr. and Nancy Elliott Edison.

Edison's parents had moved to America from Canada. Edison's father had been involved in an attempted uprising in Canada against the British, who had a lot of power and control there. Fearful of the consequences of his actions, Samuel fled Canada and traveled to America. He settled in Ohio, where he worked and made friends, including Captain Bradley.

Captain Bradley worked on barges. These large ships were used to haul goods like logs and freight up the Huron River. Captain Bradley would make trips up to Canada and back. On one of his trips to Canada, Captain Bradley returned with Nancy Edison and the Edisons' four children: Marion, William, Harriett, and Carlile. Thomas was born after the family was reunited and settled together in America.

A Curious Child

Edison was well known for his curiosity during his childhood. He was always eager to learn how things worked. However, his curiosity sometimes landed him in trouble, and even danger. There are two stories that have been popularized: one illustrates him falling into the Milan Canal and another getting caught in a grain elevator. Grain elevators were large structures similar to towers that were used for loading and storing extremely large amounts of grain. Canals were a primary means of transportation when Edison was a child. They moved people and goods from place to place. Curious about how grain elevators and the ships on the canal worked, Edison decided to investigate on these two occasions. While studying the grain elevator, he fell in but was luckily rescued before he was smothered under the grain.

Another time, he also fell into the canal. However, he was once again rescued before he became injured.

Education

Eventually, the Milan Canal was overshadowed by the railroad. The railroad was a much faster way of transporting goods and people. Soon canals, rivers, and lakes were being replaced by railroads for transportation. After the railroad arrived along the shores of Lake Erie in 1853, traffic in the Milan Canal became scarce and affected the economy of the area. Samuel Edison Jr. realized he would have to relocate in order to support his family.

In 1854, the Edison family moved north from Ohio to Port Huron, Michigan. At the age of seven, Edison attended school for the first time. His mother, Nancy, had been a schoolteacher in Canada, and she had already taught Edison to read. Edison found that he loved reading and devoured as many books as he could find. However, reading with his mother and attending school were two different things.

Not everyone embraced or appreciated Edison's childhood curiosity. Some people found him to be a pest or an annoyance, including his teachers in Port Huron. Edison would often daydream in class and find himself getting in trouble. One day, Edison overheard a conversation at his school in which he was called incapable of being taught. Edison went home and told his mother what he had heard. Nancy Edison was furious. She knew her son asked a lot of questions and could be a handful, but she also encouraged his imagination and curiosity. She rushed over to the school and defended her son. Edison's mother was so upset with the teacher and the school that she decided to teach Edison herself. This was the end of Edison's brief formal education.

Nancy Edison's defense of her son was an important moment in his life. Had she not encouraged him to keep learning and keep persisting no matter what others thought of him, he might have been tempted to give up his inquisitive ways. However, with his mother's encouragement, Edison continued reading and learning. Later in his life, after much

Edison's mother, Nancy, had a profound impact on Edison's education and career. During his lifetime, Edison largely credited his mother's encouragement for his career as an inventor.

success as an inventor, he spoke to a reporter about his mother and how much he appreciated her influence in his life:

> I did not have my mother very long but in that length of time she cast over me an influence which has lasted all of my life. The good effects of her early training I can never lose. If it had not been for her appreciation and her faith in me at a critical time in my experience, I should very likely never have become an inventor.[1]

Edison and the Railroad

Edison's family continued to struggle financially in Port Huron. Nancy Edison pitched in by sewing and weaving, and when Edison was twelve years old, he began to contribute as well. Edison took his first job working for the railroad in 1859. He was intrigued by the railroad and wanted to learn more about it. He secured a job in which he sold snacks, candies, and newspapers to train passengers, and he was allowed to keep any money he made from the sale of the items. The amount of money he made varied because it depended on how much he sold each day. Edison always gave one dollar of his daily earnings to his mother as his contribution to the family.

The Civil War

During Edison's childhood, political and social tensions had been on the rise in America. Several Southern states wanted to keep slavery, while many Northern states wanted to abolish it. Tensions rose and reached a boiling point in 1860, when Abraham Lincoln was elected the sixteenth president of the United States. Edison was thirteen years old.

Shortly after Lincoln's election, seven slave states from the South seceded and formed the Confederate States of America. When a state secedes from the rest of the country, it means the state officially declares itself no longer part of that country. The seven slave states that initially formed the Confederacy were Alabama, Florida, Georgia, Louisiana, Mississippi, South Carolina, and Texas. The Civil War officially began on April 12, 1861, with a violent battle at Fort Sumter in South Carolina. Following the violence there, an additional four states chose to secede and join the Confederacy: Arkansas, North Carolina, Tennessee, and Virginia.

The Civil War impacted Edison's life in multiple ways. Although he was too young to fight, he was well aware of what was going on because of the newspapers. Newspapers were the primary means for the public to learn new information in the 1800s. News about the war, battles, and important events would be printed and sold quickly. The public was hungry for information about the war, especially if they had loved ones who were fighting.

When Edison worked on the train, he sold newspapers and noticed how quickly the newspapers were sold and the news was consumed. Recognizing an opportunity, Edison decided to print his own newspaper. He started stopping by the newsroom to hear the latest news and then rushing to print it and sell his papers before others printed the story. He named his paper the *Weekly Herald* and printed it in the baggage car of his regular train job.

Tom the Telegrapher

The first electric telegraph message had been transmitted just three years before Edison was born, and the machine had quickly become the standard form of communication. Young Edison was fascinated by the telegraph. It was the first form of technology that Edison had witnessed, and he wanted to learn all about it. He studied telegraphy and taught himself Morse Code.

In addition to technology, Edison had discovered a love of science and began performing science experiments at home. He loved doing his experiments, even though they could be messy and sometimes scary. There would be occasional explosions. His father once said of Edison's boyhood experiments, "He will blow us all up!"[2] After several messes were made in the Edison family home, his parents made him move his laboratory to the basement.

Once Edison began working for the railroad, he found himself spending less time at home and more time on the train. Since he could not be at his basement laboratory at home, he set up another laboratory in the train's baggage car. The railroad manager allowed him to have his lab and conduct his experiments on the train. But one day, Edison conducted an experiment with chemicals, and when he mixed the chemicals together, a fire broke out on the train. The fire was extinguished and no one was hurt, but young Edison was out of a job.

Edison's career might have ended there if it weren't for another accident, this time involving the station telegrapher's son. James Mackenzie was the train station's telegrapher, the person who sent and received telegraph messages. Mackenzie had a three-year-old son who was known to play on the train tracks at the station. One day, Edison noticed a train car rolling toward the boy as he was playing. He rushed to push the boy out of the way and saved his life. Mackenzie was so grateful for Edison's quick thinking and bravery that he offered to teach

Edison professional telegraphy. Edison's telegraphy up to that point had been self-taught, and he was thrilled to be able to learn from a professional telegrapher.

In 1862, Edison began learning from Mackenzie and perfecting his Morse Code skills. He practiced for hours until he was able to send and receive Morse Code at a rate of forty-five words per minute. The standard at that time was only twenty to thirty words per minute. Edison found work as a plug telegrapher, someone who would travel to whichever telegraph office had an opening to be filled. The Civil War had created a great need for telegraphers to send and receive messages and report the news. Edison traveled all over the Midwest from one telegraph office to another.

Working at the telegraph office was a dream come true for teenage Edison. He had been fascinated by machines and the way things worked since his boyhood. Now, he had the opportunity to observe a telegraph office in person and see the machines up close. While Edison understood telegraphy and was very good at Morse Code, he found himself at a disadvantage. Telegraph machines used sound as their signals, and Edison was losing his hearing. It is unknown exactly what caused his hearing loss. It is possible it was due to a childhood illness or to trauma, such as the many falls he took as a curious boy exploring. All he knew for sure was that his hearing was weakening, and he needed to invent ways to use the telegraph that did not rely on sound alone. For this reason, the telegraph played a role in some of his very first inventions. Edison spent a lot of time in the telegraph office reading and experimenting—too much time, in fact, as he would often become so distracted that he would miss messages as they came in on the wire. As a result, he found himself fired from many telegraph offices during his career.

Much of Edison's success as an inventor was due to his work involving telegraphy. This illustration shows Edison working in a telegraph office, where he spent many hours as a young man working and inventing.

End of the War

The Civil War had served as the background for Edison's teenage years. When the war began in 1861, Edison was fourteen. The fighting ceased when Confederate commander Robert E. Lee surrendered on April 9, 1865. Less than one week later, a Confederate sympathizer named John Wilkes Booth assassinated President Abraham Lincoln. Edison was eighteen years old. Jefferson Davis, the Confederate president, tried to escape but was caught on May 10, 1865, and the Civil War was brought to an end. The issue of slavery, which largely initiated the Civil War, was put to rest on December 6, 1865, when the Thirteenth Amendment to the United States Constitution was ratified, or made official. The Thirteenth Amendment abolished slavery once and for all in the United States.

Inventions and Innovations

Following the end of the Civil War, Edison decided to pursue his passion for science. He relocated to the cities that were known for their study of science and technology, first Boston and later New York.

In 1868, Edison completed his first patent application for a machine that automatically counted votes. It was Edison's first success in that it was his first patent and first recognized invention, but it was also his first failure since it did not generate the enthusiasm and support he had hoped it would. Likewise in 1868, Edison began working for Western Union in Boston. Although he left the following year, it was not long before Edison would face the company again.

Despite the failure of his first patented invention, Edison persisted. He looked at failures as lessons. During his lifetime, he addressed his failures, stating, "I can never find the things that work best until I know the things that don't work."[3] He patented additional inventions, and in 1869, the twenty-two-year-old entrepreneur moved to New York City to devote himself to inventing full time. While in New York, Edison had friendships and even formed some business partnerships. But he was shy socially because of his hearing loss, and he quickly learned that he did not like partnerships. He did not like to be the one doing all of the work and inventing and then having other people get some of the profits.

In 1870, Edison opened his own workshop. He hired several workers, whom he fondly referred to as his boys. Many of the workers considered him a good boss who paid his employees well. Several stayed loyal to him, working in his workshop for years. However, there were others who worked for Edison only briefly, including Serbian immigrant Nikola Tesla. Tesla began working for Edison in 1884 but quit in 1885 over a payment dispute, and the two later became bitter rivals.

Edison worked long days and through many nights with his workers, spending days at a time in his workshop. His reputation as an inventor was growing, but he still had not found his fame and fortune.

Around 1874, Edison created a new version of the telegraph, known as Edison's quadruplex. The device could send four different telegraph messages at once, two in each direction. It was a revolution. Edison gained interest in the invention from his former employer, Western Union, and even had a team at the company assembled to operate the device. He had also agreed to share inventor status with one of Western Union's chief electricians. However, after paying him for only part of his work, Western Union apparently did not follow through on its promises.

Edison soon found a different financial backer. Jay Gould was a man made wealthy by the railroad industry. He was also interested in the telegraphy business. Gould offered Edison $30,000 (around $663,000 in 2018) as the first payment for his new invention. This fee was much higher than Western Union's offer. Edison accepted, and it seemed as though he was finally making money and earning a reputation as an inventor.

Family Life

Family had always been important to Edison, particularly his mother. In 1871, Edison's mother passed away. After attending her funeral in Port Huron, he traveled back to New York to throw himself into his work.

Edison deeply felt the loss of his mother, and it was perhaps this loss that contributed to his desire to be married and have a family of his own. Although his hearing loss made him self-conscious around women, he did desire to have a wife and children. Upon returning to work after his mother's funeral, Edison found himself interested in one of his own factory workers, a young woman named Mary Stilwell. Stilwell was only sixteen years old when Edison approached her in a businesslike manner and asked her if she would be interested in becoming his wife. The two were married on Christmas Day, 1871, when Stilwell was sixteen and Edison was twenty-four. The newlyweds made their home in Newark, New Jersey, but it was primarily Mary who tended to the house, while Edison spent most of his time in his workshop.

Edison's desire for a family was realized when he and Mary welcomed three children. Their daughter, Marion, was born in 1873, and Thomas Alva Edison Jr. was born in 1876. Much of Edison's career and success up to that point could be attributed to the telegraph and Morse Code. Edison jokingly nicknamed his daughter Marion "Dot" and his son Thomas Jr. "Dash" as a nod to the invention and code that had had such an impact on his life. Edison and Mary's third and last child together was a boy named William Leslie Edison, born in 1878.

Marriage and family life did not change Edison's work habits. He continued to work for days and nights at a time, sleeping little, and spending most of his time in his workshop.

Menlo Park

In the late 1870s, Edison decided he wanted to get out of the city, believing he would be able to concentrate more clearly in a quiet place. He bought land in Menlo Park, New Jersey, where he built a farmhouse for his family and a two-story laboratory. In 1876, he moved his laboratory to the new Menlo Park location. Edison and his boys had a lot of fun in the Menlo Park laboratory. They played music, sang songs, and told jokes. They also worked hard and often, earning a reputation as the lab that never slept.

The Phonograph

The Menlo Park laboratory was the birthplace of Edison's most famous inventions. It was at Menlo Park that he recorded and replayed the human voice for the first time in 1877, though historians debate about the exact date. Using his new invention, called the phonograph, Edison recorded himself reciting the popular children's rhyme "Mary Had a Little Lamb." America and the rest of the world were amazed at the invention. Never before had the human voice been recorded and played back. Edison demonstrated his phonograph for the public and in Washington, DC, for Congress and President Rutherford B. Hayes.

Let There Be Light

Following the phonograph was Edison's most well-known and celebrated invention, the electric lightbulb. While electricity had existed for some time, no one had yet created a long-lasting lightbulb that could work for an extended period of time and was safe to use. Several inventors had been working on an inexpensive, long-lasting lightbulb that would

Edison is seen here in 1878 with one of his phonograph machines. Edison's phonograph was his first big invention that launched his inventing career.

be available for consumers to purchase, but no one had yet figured out how to make it.

Edison began working on an electric lightbulb and, realizing he was on the cusp of something big, formed the Edison Electric Light Company in 1878. Years later, after a series of mergers, this company would evolve into the General Electric Company, which still exists today.

Edison tried many attempts at creating an electric lightbulb, but they all burned out or burned up. However, he did not stop trying. He had once stated to a reporter about one of his inventions, "I have not failed. I've just found 10,000 ways that won't work."[4] Finally, on October 21, 1879, Edison successfully burned an electric lightbulb for over a day. On January 27, 1880, he filed another patent, this time for an incandescent lightbulb that would bring electric lighting inside buildings and homes and revolutionize the world. An incandescent lightbulb is a small glass globe that looks similar to lightbulbs we see today. Electricity generates heat inside the globe, and the heat then creates light.

Edison didn't have much time to enjoy his victory. Before long, other inventors were offering their own means of electricity to consumers. Inventors George Westinghouse and Nikola Tesla, who had once been Edison's employee, became engaged in an all-out war with him when they introduced a new type of electric current. To likewise challenge Edison, Westinghouse formed his own electric company, the Westinghouse Electric Company, in 1886. It would go up against Edison's electric company. An ugly rivalry ensued, and Edison spent years battling Westinghouse and Tesla over the electricity market.

Lights, Camera, Action!

By the late 1800s, inventors had created ways to capture images in photographs and record sound. However, nobody had been

THE POWER OF THE PRESS

Being famous in the 1800s looked very different than it does today. Before radio, television, and computers, the newspaper was the main source of information for the public. Being featured in the newspaper was how people became famous or infamous (meaning well known for doing something bad).

During the nineteenth century, newspapers and magazines were often dedicated to a particular topic or area of interest, such as science, politics, or finance. Popular magazines included *Telegrapher*, dedicated to news pertaining to telegraph operators, and *Scientific American*, dedicated to science and technology, which is still in circulation today. Popular newspapers included the *Washington Globe* and the *New York Journal of Commerce*.

Edison had had a relationship with newspapers since his boyhood, when he sold newspapers on the train and even printed his own newspaper. He knew the power of the press from an early age. For inventors like him, how the newspapers reported on you and your inventions could make or break your reputation and career. The press had tremendous influence over the public, and if they reported favorably about you, it could lead to fame and investments in your business. If they reported negatively, it could end your career.

After inventing the phonograph in 1877, Edison received an enormous amount of press coverage. Reporters crowded Edison's Menlo Park laboratory hoping for interviews, statements, and demonstrations of his latest experiments. Edison played along, using the press as a means to get exposure, fame, and financial investments. It was the press who propelled Edison from an inventor to watch to one of the great inventors of the day. In fact, it was the *New York Daily Graphic* that dubbed him "the Wizard of Menlo Park."[5]

After the frenzy of the phonograph, Edison found himself exhausted by the press coverage and the fame. Still, he knew he would need positive press coverage for future inventions and did not want to become estranged from the press. As he worked on his next invention, the incandescent lightbulb, he made it a point to invite the press for demonstrations. The positive press coverage he received granted him financial investments and additional fame.

CHAPTER THREE

Friendships and Rivalries

Thomas Edison was just one of several inventors and entrepreneurs who earned their fame and fortune during the nineteenth and twentieth centuries. The invention of the electric telegraph ushered in a new era of technology, and many scientists and inventors were eager to create the next innovation that would change the world. Edison counted some fellow inventors and entrepreneurs as friends, including automobile maker Henry Ford. However, he also had some competitors and enemies.

Edison is pictured here with fellow inventor and friend Henry Ford.

Henry Ford

Henry Ford was an American inventor born on July 30, 1863, in Wayne County, Michigan. When Ford was born, Thomas Edison was sixteen and getting his first glimpse at a professional telegraph office. He was also starting to think about inventions that might improve the process. As Ford grew up, he, along with the rest of the world, watched in awe as Edison began his career as an inventor, improving upon the telegraph, recording the human voice, and pursuing an electric lightbulb. Ford greatly admired Edison and aspired to be an inventor himself one day.

In 1891, Ford had the opportunity to work for Edison at one of Edison's electric power plants in Detroit, Michigan. That same year, he completed his first gasoline engine as part of his vision for creating a gasoline-powered automobile. In 1893, Ford was promoted to chief engineer at Edison's power plant. Three years later, he got the opportunity to meet Edison in person at a convention in Brooklyn, New York, in 1896. The two men had great respect for one another and formed a friendship that lasted the rest of their lives.

Ford spent years working on his automobile design, occasionally consulting with Edison on his ideas and plans. In 1908, Ford changed the world when he introduced the Model T, which still remains one of the best-selling automobiles of all time. By 1913, Ford had changed the face of manufacturing by introducing his assembly line. Rather than having one person perform multiple tasks that were time consuming, the assembly line assigned just one task to each person. Ford also built machines that were capable of performing tasks faster than people could perform them. Ford's assembly line made the production of automobiles much faster and much less expensive.

The friendship between Ford and Edison remained strong up until Edison's death. Over the years, the two inventors enjoyed vacation homes near one another in Florida, went on camping trips with mutual friends, and sent birthday greetings and letters to one another. Ford even helped Edison financially when it was needed. In 1914, Edison suffered a great financial loss after a devastating fire broke out in one of his concrete labs. Ford was there to bail out his friend, loaning him the money needed to rebuild. Edison and Ford's friendship is an example of two men in the same field who were able to support and learn from one another, rather than act as competitors or rivals.

Alexander Graham Bell

On March 3, 1847, about three weeks after Thomas Edison was born in Milan, Ohio, Alexander Graham Bell was born in Edinburgh, Scotland. By the time Bell was twenty-three years old, he had moved with his family to multiple countries, including England and Canada. Bell received his education from many different schools, including University College London, but he never completed his studies due to the family's frequent moves. In 1871, Bell moved to Boston, Massachusetts, where he began the first of several teaching jobs at various schools for the deaf. Bell's mother, Eliza, had been nearly deaf, and Bell's father, Alexander, had taught speech to the deaf. Bell was carrying on the family career, which was a cause near to their hearts.

While teaching, Bell also spent time pursuing his other passion, technology. He had a particular focus on telegraphy and began experimenting with ways to improve the process by sending multiple messages over a single wire at one time. Bell wasn't the only inventor to pursue such a goal. In 1868, Joseph Stearns beat Bell to the punch when he invented the duplex.

Alexander Graham Bell, seen here in his later life, was a fellow inventor alongside Edison in the nineteenth and twentieth centuries. The two remained rivals throughout their careers.

The duplex was a way to send two messages at one time over a single telegraph wire. Thomas Edison would later improve upon Stearns's duplex by inventing the quadruplex in 1874. The quadruplex allowed four messages to be sent simultaneously over a single telegraph wire.

After being defeated by Stearns and Edison, Bell decided to focus his attention on sending messages using the human voice rather than telegraphs. On February 14, 1876, he filed a patent for his device that could transmit sounds like musical notes. Bell believed his device could be used to transmit the human voice as well. Yet again, Bell wasn't the only inventor working on transmitting sound. Another inventor and rival of Bell's was Elisha Gray. Just hours after Bell filed his patent for what would become the telephone, Gray filed a statement in which he described a similar device that he planned to produce for the same purpose. Bell and Gray became locked in a legal battle over who had the rights to the invention. On March 7, 1876, Bell received the rights to what has been called "one of the most valuable patents in history."[1] He continued his work, and on March 10, 1876, the first telephone call was made to Bell's assistant, Thomas A. Watson, saying, "Mr. Watson—come here—I want to see you."[2]

Bell and Edison crossed paths throughout their careers as inventors. Edison, who was competitive by nature, considered Bell his rival. Edison was even hired by Western Union to compete with Bell. Western Union wanted Edison to create a machine similar to Bell's telephone, but Bell's patents prevented him from doing so.

The two inventors would continue to encounter one another throughout their careers, even improving upon each other's inventions. In 1886, Bell patented his graphophone, an improved version of Edison's phonograph. The year after Bell's

THE UNITED STATES PATENT SYSTEM

Shortly after founding their new country, the Founding Fathers realized the need for inventors, artists, and authors to be able to protect their work. Patents were created to officially declare that the rights to an invention belonged to the person who spent the time developing and creating it. The Patent Act was passed on April 10, 1790, and was signed by President George Washington. The Patent Act stated that a patent could be issued for "any useful art, manufacture, engine, machine, or device, or any improvement thereon not before known or used."[3]

The US Patent Office was formed and included a patent board. The board members handled the issuing of the patents. Thomas Jefferson, then secretary of state and future US president, was a member of the first patent board. He acted as administrator and reviewed patent applications.

The first US patent was issued to Samuel Hopkins of Philadelphia, Pennsylvania. The patent was for an improvement to the process of making an ingredient used in fertilizer. The patent was issued on July 31, 1790, and signed by President George Washington.

Patents played a crucial role in the work of inventors like Thomas Edison. So many inventors were working on similar devices and machines that it was very important to protect their work with patents. Without a patent to protect his work, Edison's ideas could have been stolen and his inventions reproduced by someone else who would then profit off of his creativity and hard work. Edison applied for his first patent in 1868 and was awarded the patent in 1869. It was for his automatic vote-counting machine. In total, Edison held 1,093 patents in the United States, and at one time, he held the record for the most patents issued to any one person.

The US Patent and Trademark Office still exists today to protect the work of artists, inventors, and entrepreneurs. While patents protect ideas and inventions, trademarks protect phrases, slogans, and symbols. Millions of patents have been issued since Samuel Hopkins received the first one in 1790. On June 19, 2018, the United States Patent and Trademark Office issued its ten millionth patent.

famous first phone call, Edison invented the microphone, which improved upon Bell's telephone. Prior to the microphone, telephone users had to shout to be heard by the person on the other end. Edison's microphone allowed people to speak in normal tones on the phone. Despite these improvements to one another's inventions, Edison and Bell remained rivals throughout their careers.

The War of the Currents

Like Edison, George Westinghouse was an inventor in late nineteenth-century America. Like Bell, Westinghouse was Edison's competition. Westinghouse was born the year before Edison, on October 6, 1846, in Central Bridge, New York.

The rivalry between Edison and Westinghouse went beyond two men in the same occupation striving to come up with the next big advancement in technology. Westinghouse and Edison became involved in a famous feud over electricity. It was called the War of the Currents.

George Westinghouse received over one hundred patents during his career as an inventor and found success with inventions for the railroad. In 1869, Westinghouse patented an air brake for trains that was so successful in improving train safety that it became mandatory on all American trains.

It was Westinghouse's work on trains and railroads that introduced him to different types of electrical currents. There was direct current, which delivered a consistent amount of electricity, and alternating current, which could reduce the amount of electricity being sent to certain structures like homes. While Edison used direct current, alternating current had become popular in Europe. Intrigued, Westinghouse did some research and decided that alternating current was the better choice. In

1886, he created the Westinghouse Electric Company, a direct competitor to Edison's own electric company, which used direct current. But Westinghouse didn't just start his own competing electric company. He also hired one of Edison's former workers to be his employee and help him improve his power system.

Nikola Tesla

Nikola Tesla was a Serbian inventor born on July 10, 1856, in what is now Croatia. Tesla immigrated to America on June 6, 1884. Like most immigrants of the time, Tesla entered America through New York City. Upon his arrival, he went to work for Edison. Tesla fit in well with Edison's boys, working long days and sleepless nights to perfect Edison's inventions. Years later, in a 1931 interview with the *New York Times*, Tesla described his brief period of working for Edison:

> We experimented day and night, holidays not excepted. His existence was made up of alternate periods of work and sleep in the laboratory. He had no hobby, cared for no sport or amusement of any kind and lived in utter disregard of the most elementary rules of hygiene ... so great and uncontrollable was his passion for work.[4]

Tesla did not stay employed with Edison for very long. He quit working for him in 1885 over a dispute regarding pay. Edison had told Tesla that he could expect a nice bonus if he was able to make one of Edison's electric generators more productive for less cost. Tesla succeeded, but when he asked Edison for his bonus money, Edison said that the bonus had been a joke. Tesla parted ways with Edison and struck out on his own.

Nikola Tesla briefly worked for Edison before striking out on his own. He later partnered with George Westinghouse, and a bitter battle with Edison over electricity ensued.

The system of electricity that Edison had designed used direct current. This means that the same amount of electricity flows in one direction at all times. Tesla designed a different kind of electrical system called alternating current. This means that the direction of the electricity alternates, or changes back and forth. As a result of the alternation, it is easier to change the strength of the current, rather than sending out one large amount of electricity continuously. Alternating current could reduce the amount of electricity being sent to buildings and homes while still sending large amounts of electricity where it was needed, such as factories and industrial buildings. Edison's direct current, however, could only send the same amount of electricity at all times to all places. Edison's direct current could only be sent over short distances, so many power plants were needed to provide electricity to customers. Alternating current, however, was able to travel over long distances, making fewer power plants necessary. This means it was less expensive to produce alternating current and therefore, Westinghouse could charge his customers less money for electricity than Edison could.

In 1888, Tesla sold patents for his alternating-current system and technologies to George Westinghouse. The team challenged Edison directly and rapidly gained customers. Alternating current was not only less expensive than Edison's direct current, but it was also considered a much safer option for electricity since the voltage, or amount of electricity being sent, could be reduced for homes.

Afraid of losing his customers to Westinghouse and Tesla, Edison began a smear campaign to discredit them. In Edison's case, he wanted to portray alternating current as dangerous. Edison's direct current electrical wires had been built underground, but Westinghouse had built his electrical wires above ground with the wires strung up in the air. Edison started proclaiming the dangers of the Westinghouse wires, stating that they could potentially fall and injure or even kill someone. Edison also began public demonstrations of electrocutions using alternating current to show how dangerous it was. He even electrocuted stray dogs in public to make his point.

In retaliation against Edison, Westinghouse launched his own smear campaign. He boasted about the Westinghouse safety record and claimed that Edison's electrical system had been responsible for multiple fires.

Edison was hoping that alternating current would be considered so dangerous it would be made illegal, leaving room for only his direct current to provide electricity. He even went so far as to suggest that alternating current could become a new form of execution by creating an electric chair. On August 6, 1890, a convicted killer named William Kemmler was the first person executed by electric chair. Edison hoped he could defeat Westinghouse and Tesla by getting people to associate alternating current electricity with death.

Despite Edison's efforts to portray alternating current as dangerous to the public, Westinghouse and Tesla persisted. By 1889, Westinghouse had amassed around five times as many customers as Edison had. In 1893, Edison was dealt the final blow of the war of the currents when Westinghouse and Tesla were chosen instead of Edison to build a hydroelectric power plant at Niagara Falls., New York. Tesla went on to build the first hydroelectric power plant, using the rushing waters of Niagara Falls as an electricity generator. On November 16, 1896, Tesla's hydroelectric power plant switched on, illuminating the city of Buffalo, New York. Alternating current had won the war of the currents, and it is still the standard type of electricity used in homes today.

CHAPTER FOUR

Innovative Inventions

In the late nineteenth and early twentieth centuries, the name Thomas Edison became synonymous with science and technology. From his laboratory in Menlo Park, Edison produced multiple inventions that changed the world. Most notably, he recorded and played back the human voice for the first time, invented the incandescent lightbulb, and captured the first motion picture. But what led Edison to pursue his inventions? How did he go about inventing them, and what obstacles did he overcome in the process?

Edison's lightbulb brought electric lighting indoors.

Capturing Sound

Edison is perhaps most well known for his invention of the incandescent lamp, or electric lightbulb. However, he invented a number of things that advanced technology and changed the world. While the phonograph was not his first invention, it was the first invention that propelled Edison into the spotlight as an inventor to watch and made him famous throughout the world.

An Unintended Invention

Edison did not set out to invent the phonograph but created it out of his efforts to improve two other famous inventions, the telegraph and the telephone. He wanted to be able to print out telegraph and telephone messages. He thought that the two types of message could possibly be printed out in the same way if he could somehow capture what was being sent and what was being spoken. He focused his attentions on trying to create a machine that could do this.

Edison began experimenting with the diaphragm, or the speaking part, of the telephone. He attached a point to the diaphragm that would vibrate when he spoke. The vibrations from Edison's voice caused the point to make etches onto paper. Edison was hoping to take the paper etches from the speaking vibrations and play back what he had just said.

During his experiments, Edison made some adjustments and tried different things. He switched the paper for a metal cylinder and wrapped it in tin foil. He began to use two diaphragms, each with a needle of its own. One diaphragm and needle were used to record what he was saying onto the metal cylinder. The other diaphragm and needle ideally would be used to play back what he had just said.

While experimenting with an early telephone, like the one pictured here, Edison recorded and played back his own voice. This led to the invention of the phonograph.

Edison tested his new invention by speaking a traditional children's nursery rhyme into the diaphragm. He said, "Mary had a little lamb."[1] When he played back the cylinder, he heard himself speaking the nursery rhyme. Edison had become the first person to capture sound and play it back. The date that he made this first official recording and replay of the human voice is debated. Some historians place this occurrence in August 1877 while others place it later, in December 1877. He did not file a patent for his phonograph machine until December 24, 1877, so the later date for his invention is often considered more accurate. Edison received the official patent for his phonograph on February 19, 1878.

World Fame

Edison decided to take his new invention to the offices of *Scientific American* in New York City. He shared his phonograph with the staff, and at first, they thought he was joking. They didn't think he had actually found a way to record and play back the human voice. So Edison did a demonstration for the staff in which he played his own voice speaking to them. The office staff were amazed, and *Scientific American* featured him and his new phonograph machine in the December 22, 1877 issue, saying:

> Mr. Thomas A. Edison recently came into this office, placed a little machine on our desk, turned a crank, and the machine inquired as to our health, asked how we liked the phonograph, informed us that it was very well, and bid us a cordial good night.[2]

Other magazines and newspapers began reporting on Edison and his phonograph, and he quickly became famous throughout the world. Edison had high hopes for the future of his invention, and on January 24, 1878, he formed the Edison Speaking Phonograph Company.

The Future of the Phonograph

Edison had many ideas for how his phonograph could be used in the future. He thought that it would be useful for offices, especially for dictation. Dictation is when someone speaks aloud words that they would like written down, such as letters and professional correspondence. Edison thought the phonograph could be a way to reproduce music, record books for the blind to listen to, create music boxes and add

Alexander Graham Bell attempted to improve upon Edison's phonograph by inventing the graphophone, pictured here. Edison was furious and refused to work with Bell.

sound to toys, capture lessons and lectures in classrooms, and preserve languages.

Many of Edison's ideas are still commonly used today. Recording music, classroom lectures, and audiobooks are all common and popular practices. But this is largely because the technology behind these recordings has been perfected over the years. Unfortunately for Edison, when his phonograph was invented and introduced to the public in the late 1800s, it was difficult to use. Edison's phonograph could not record for very long, and the tin foil used to play back the recording was not very durable. It gave out after just a few playings.

Due to these setbacks, Edison chose to step back from his phonograph and shifted his focus to the electric lightbulb. As he stepped back from the phonograph, his longtime competitor, Alexander Graham Bell, decided to take a closer look at the machine. He began to work with his cousin and a fellow scientist to try to improve it. One of the big changes they made was replacing Edison's tin foil with wax. On May 4, 1886, they were rewarded for their efforts with a patent for what they called a graphophone. When asked if he would consider working with Bell and his associates on this new, improved version of the phonograph, Edison refused. He also refused the half share he was offered in the American Graphophone Company, stating, "Under no circumstances will I have anything to do with Graham Bell [or] with his phonograph pronounced backward."[3]

The Fate of the Phonograph

Years later, after he invented the incandescent lightbulb, Edison decided to return to his phonograph. Rather than work alongside Bell or take part ownership of his company, he worked to improve the phonograph on his own. On October 8, 1887, Edison formed the Edison Phonograph Company and introduced his new phonograph. Edison's new phonograph largely followed Bell's graphophone, replacing Edison's original tin foil-wrapped metal cylinders with wax cylinders.

Edison decided to pursue some of his original ideas for the phonograph and began marketing his machine to be used for dictation in offices. But this caused a lot of backlash from stenographers, who noted words, phrases, even whole letters or books, from speech to paper. They were often employed in offices to write down letters, memos, and other correspondence. With the introduction of the phonograph, stenographers were at risk of losing their jobs.

In 1890, Edison tried to make another idea a reality with the Edison Phonograph Toy Manufacturing Company. Edison's company began making talking dolls using phonographs. A small phonograph cylinder with prerecorded sayings on it was placed inside each doll. Unfortunately, the dolls were very delicate and often broke during shipment. It seemed Edison's vision for the phonograph was once again shattered, this time along with the talking dolls.

Edison's phonograph went through many stages and growing pains until finally being formed into a machine that was easy to use and affordable. In 1905, an improved version was introduced. This one was easier for secretaries to use and became popular in offices and with businesses. By 1916, an even further improved version, called the Ediphone, became popular and began to increase in sales. Nearly forty years after Edison first recorded himself reciting a children's nursery rhyme, it had finally been turned into an affordable, marketable, and popular product.

A Bright Idea

Following his fame from the phonograph, Edison next set his sights on creating an electric lightbulb that would be long-lasting, safe, and affordable for the public.

Before Edison's lightbulb and electrical system, gas lighting was used to illuminate streets, buildings, and homes. However, gas lamps were expensive, with mostly only wealthy citizens being able to afford them for their homes. This meant that most people lost light when the sun went down. Edison set out to create an affordable and safe electric lightbulb that could be used in homes, buildings, and on streets to light up entire cities.

Since the discovery of electricity, people had been attempting to harness its power for various uses. In the 1800s, many people tried to use electricity for indoor and outdoor lighting. One kind of lighting that existed was called arc lighting, or arc lamps. In 1876, an American inventor named Moses Farmer displayed an arc light at the Centennial Exposition in Philadelphia, Pennsylvania. The Centennial Exposition was also the first World's Fair, a place where inventors and scientists could demonstrate their newest inventions and technologies. People attending the exposition expected to see the technology of the future. Farmer's arc light was something that amazed many people. An arc light was a type of electric light that used electricity to create a curved light, or arc, between two carbon rods. Arc lights were very bright, which made them popular for lighting large areas like streets. However, their brightness also made them impractical for lighting homes and buildings.

Scientists and inventors realized that arc lighting was not the way to bring electric lighting indoors. Many began working on indoor lighting technologies, including British inventor Joseph Swan, English chemist Humphry Davy, and Canadian

Before Edison invented his lightbulb, arc lamps, like the one pictured here, were a form of electric lighting commonly used. However, arc lamps created extremely bright lights, making them a poor choice for indoor lighting.

inventors Henry Woodward and Mathew Evans. Most of them set their sights on incandescent lightbulbs. An incandescent lightbulb is lit through heat. Inventors from around the globe were trying their hand at creating indoor electric lighting. The first patent granted for an incandescent lightbulb went to English inventor Frederick de Moleyns in 1841.

The problem with early incandescent lightbulbs was that while they worked and produced light, they burned out too quickly. The strip of material inside the bulb that became heated to produce light did not last long. The heat quickly caused the strips to burn up or melt.

Like other inventors of his time, Edison often found himself trying to improve upon previous inventions, to make something new from an idea or invention that already existed. He famously said of his work on his inventions, "I start where the last man left off."[4] Edison meant that he would attempt to improve upon existing inventions, moving them forward and advancing their technology. Edison's lightbulb was no exception.

Edison's Improvements

Once Edison set his sights on the incandescent lightbulb, he paid a visit to Moses Farmer's factory in 1878. Edison found himself inspired and hurried home to Menlo Park to begin his work. Edison was overconfident, or some might say arrogant, when he promised to invent a working, safe, and affordable electric lightbulb within six weeks. Edison set to work in his laboratory studying and experimenting. He soon realized the electric lightbulb wasn't going to come easily or quickly.

Edison had developed good relationships with reporters and newspapers, and he used these relationships to his benefit. He gave reporters information about his experiments and demonstrated one of his early lightbulb models. This brought Edison favorable reports in the news, which led to financial investments that he needed to fund his work. In October 1878, the Edison Electric Light Company was established, and Edison was convinced he was on the verge of a breakthrough.

He tried using multiple materials to act as the filament, or strip, that gets heated inside the lightbulb. But everything he tried burned up or melted. This was the same problem that had kept inventors scratching their heads for decades. Edison tried covering and protecting the filament inside a small globe, or vacuum, within the larger bulb. But that didn't work either. Convinced it must be the material, Edison kept trying different types, waiting to find the right one. Finally, on October 21, 1879, he tried using cotton thread that had been carbonized as his filament. He placed the filament inside a vacuum within a glass globe. When the globe was attached to an electric battery, it began to give off light. Afraid that this filament would burn up like the others, Edison and his boys watched the light hour after hour. This time, it didn't burn out. In fact, it glowed for over a day. Edison had finally done what so many had tried to do before him. He had created a practical, electric, incandescent lightbulb.

By the end of 1879, Edison was ready to demonstrate his new invention to the public. On New Year's Eve, he used over four hundred electric bulbs to light the streets and houses of Menlo Park, as well as his laboratory. Seeing entire streets and cities lit up with electric lighting is common now and often is not even reflected upon. However, in the late nineteenth century, the sight of hundreds of lightbulbs illuminating multiple homes and streets was something that had not been viewed before. It was breathtaking and furthered Edison's reputation as an inventor who had and would continue to change the world.

The First Power Plant

Creating the first practical electric lightbulb was only step one for Edison. He soon realized that in order for the lightbulb to be of any use, it would need an electrical source to connect to. Electricity today is not at all like it was in Edison's day. There were no light switches, on and off power switches, electrical wires, or power companies to supply homes with the electricity needed to turn on Edison's lightbulbs. In order to make his new lightbulb truly useful in homes, Edison was going to have to build an entire electrical system to go along with it.

Edison set his sights on downtown Manhattan. He purchased property on Pearl Street, which he turned into

FILMING THE SPANISH-AMERICAN WAR

In 1888, Thomas Edison had begun working on a new invention, a motion-picture camera. Edison described his work, saying, "I am experimenting upon an instrument which does for the eye what the phonograph does for the ear, which is the recording and reproduction of things in motion."[5]

In 1891, Edison invented a camera that could record motion. He called his invention the kinetograph. Edison realized that once motion was recorded, he would need another device to play it back so he could watch what he had just captured. In 1897, Edison patented his kinetoscope, a device with a small viewing hole through which he could view the motion picture he had recorded with his kinetograph. Edison produced the first motion picture ever to be copyrighted in 1894 when he filmed one of his employees sneezing. The film was black and white, silent, and lasted only three seconds. Four years later, Edison's motion picture camera had been developed further and was used for capturing much more significant events than sneezes.

On April 25, 1898, America declared war with Spain over Spain's rule in Cuba and other islands. The Cubans had been fighting for independence from Spain for years, and America had declared that it would remain neutral. This changed on February 15, 1898, when the American battleship USS *Maine* was sunk in Havana. The war was a struggle for Spain. Americans overtook Spanish fleets, destroying and sinking their ships. The war was short, ending on December 10, 1898, with the signing of the Treaty of Paris, in which Spain gave up control of Cuba.

Edison's motion-picture camera played a significant role in the Spanish-American War. It was the first war in which a motion-picture camera was used to capture actual footage of the war in America, Cuba, and the Philippines. The Edison Manufacturing Company and the American Mutoscope & Biograph Company produced footage showing troops, ships, and parades. They also produced reenactments of important battles. This was the first time that the public was able to see real footage of a war that was being fought across the ocean in other countries.

Today, it's an everyday occurrence to view news coverage and footage of different countries, wars, important political figures, and significant social events and gatherings. However, in the late nineteenth century, the motion-picture camera and this kind of coverage of important events were revolutionary, just as Edison's phonograph and lightbulb had been previously. Watching footage produced by Edison's company amazed people, and the public's interest in viewing this kind of footage helped to create the visual news reports and coverage we know and expect today.

Edison's Menlo Park laboratory, reproduced here as part of a museum, was where Edison spent long days and nights working toward his most famous inventions.

a lightbulb factory and the first electric power plant. He determined that it would be safer to run his power lines and electrical wires underground rather than have them installed aboveground. However, it wasn't until 1881 that the city of New York granted him permission to dig. After years of working

Edison's dream of illuminating Manhattan with his lightbulbs was realized in 1882. This illustration shows some of the first street lighting on Fifth Avenue in Manhattan.

to invent the electric lightbulb and then building an electrical system to power the lightbulb, Edison's dream was realized on September 4, 1882, when he successfully illuminated 1 square mile (2.6 square kilometers) of downtown Manhattan in New York City.

Edison's inventions took years of work to create and then many more to perfect. Today, we take many things like electricity and music recordings for granted. In Edison's day, though, the phonograph and the electric lightbulb were revolutionary and are two of the reasons he is considered one of the greatest inventors and scientists of all time.

will at least delay anybody's purchasing until your system can be seen.[1]

Gouraud was hoping to promote Edison's new electrical system over gas systems in Europe so financial backers would be willing to fund Edison's work instead of investing in gas companies. Gas lighting companies were not pleased with the publicity Edison was getting surrounding his upcoming electric lighting system. They feared Edison's new invention would put them out of business and began a smear campaign stating the dangers of electricity and why gas was a safer option. It was not unlike the smear campaign Edison would later use against his rivals Westinghouse and Tesla. In response to the smear campaign, Edison launched one of his own about the dangers of using gas lighting and why electricity was the safer option.

Edison's lightbulb impacted more than just stocks and investments. Once indoor electric lighting became widely available, people no longer had to set their work schedules by daylight. Before electric lighting, people had to stop working when it got dark outside. This included factory workers. But once indoor electric lighting was available in factories, workers were able to stay longer and work more hours a day. While this created long days for workers, factory owners were pleased because it increased their productivity. They were able to produce much more product in a shorter amount of time.

Edison's indoor electric lighting allowed for more than just longer workdays. Factories had caused urbanization to occur, and then Edison's indoor lighting caused urbanization to flourish. Cities were soon alive well after dark, offering entertainment to children and adults. Social gatherings could take place at night, such as dances. Parks, ballgames, concerts, and taverns all offered nighttime entertainment. Previously darkened city

THOMAS PAINE, PHILOSOPHER AND INVENTOR

Thomas Paine was an English writer, philosopher, and inventor who lived during the eighteenth century. Some of his works include the essays "The Age of Reason," "Rights of Man," and "Common Sense." While Paine's writings were philosophical, they were also often political in nature. Paine's essay "Common Sense" was published during the American Revolution and discussed the importance of the colonists declaring independence from Britain. "Common Sense" was very influential with the Founding Fathers, most notably Thomas Jefferson, the author of the Declaration of Independence.

Although Paine died nearly forty years before Edison was born, Edison considered him a role model. Edison discovered Paine through his father, who had a collection of Paine's writings. Edison's father encouraged him to read that collection when he was a boy. Edison was so convinced of the importance and relevance of Paine's work that he penned an essay about the importance of it in 1925 titled "The Philosophy of Thomas Paine by Thomas Edison." In his essay, he expressed Paine's influence over his own life:

> I have always been interested in this man. My father had a set of Tom Paine's books on the shelf at home. I must have opened the covers about the time I was 13. And I can still remember the flash of enlightenment which shone from his pages. It was a revelation, indeed, to encounter his views on political and religious matters, so different from the views of many people around us. Of course I did not understand him very well, but his sincerity and ardor made an impression upon me that nothing has ever served to lessen ...

Thomas Paine influenced Edison throughout his life. This bust of him appears in New Rochelle, New York.

I was always interested in Paine the inventor. He conceived and designed the iron bridge and the hollow candle; the principle of the modern central draught burner. The man had a sort of universal genius. He was interested in a diversity of things; but his special creed, his first thought, was liberty.[2]

Edison's essay regarding Paine's work was his way of paying tribute to one of his role models. Paine's writings first inspired the Founding Fathers in their fight to form a new nation. He later inspired one of that very nation's most successful and most prolific inventors.

streets were illuminated, offering an exciting new world to the city's residents. Edison's electric lighting had transformed daily life and created a new industry of nighttime entertainment. The entertainment was not only fun for people to attend, but it created a whole new source of revenue, or income, for the business owners, towns, and cities.

Edison's Critics

While many people were amazed at Edison's inventions and considered him a technology wizard, others were less impressed and even skeptical. After Edison invented the phonograph, there was much publicity about it. Many newspapers ran favorable stories while others ran less favorable ones, questioning the usefulness of Edison's inventions, suggesting they might do more harm than good, and even questioning his character. One example is the following article that ran in the *New York Times* on March 25, 1878:

> Mr. Edison has invented too many things, and almost without exception they are things of the most deleterious character. He has been addicted to electricity for many years, and it is not very long ago that he became notorious for having discovered a new force, though he has since kept it carefully concealed, either upon his person or elsewhere. Recently, he invented the phonograph, a machine that catches the lightest whisper of conversation and stores it up, so that at any future time it can be brought out, to the confusion of the original speaker. This machine will eventually destroy all confidence between man and man, and render more dangerous than ever woman's want of confidence in woman.[3]

This reporter was making fun of Edison, depicting him as a kind of madman who invented due to his obsession with electricity and his desire to create machines that may stir up trouble for others. The phonograph is depicted in this article as something dangerous, something that could be used for negative means such as possibly recording people without their knowledge and then later playing it back to confuse and manipulate them.

Edison's fame made him an easy target for the press. Another example of the press having fun at his expense was an

THE ELECTRIC LIGHT.

Some newspapers poked fun at Edison, like this cartoon from 1880. Edison (*left*) is depicted as joining hands with Charles F. Brush (*right*), who perfected and promoted the arc light, rather than inventing a light of his own.

April Fool's Day hoax published by the *New York Daily Graphic* on April 1, 1878. The newspaper article claimed that Edison had solved world hunger by inventing a machine called a food creator. Edison's food creator, the article claimed, could turn water into wine and soil into foods like biscuits, meats, and vegetables. Many people believed the article, and it was, in fact, reprinted by other newspapers, spreading the word of Edison's latest invention. The hoax poked fun at Edison but also at those who believed he truly was some kind of wizard who could invent anything and solve any problem.

Stolen Inventions

Criticism of Edison's work existed not only during Edison's lifetime but continues today in the twenty-first century. Several articles, books, and videos have been dedicated to the idea that Edison was not the scientific genius that many credit him as, but was in fact a thief who stole the ideas and inventions of others. One example is Edison's phonograph, which some say he stole from Frenchman Edouard-Leon Scott de Martinville, who captured sound years before Edison. Scott invented the phonautograph, his device for recording sound, in 1857, twenty years before Edison invented his phonograph. While some say Edison stole the idea from Scott, Edison was always open about his process of conducting research based on previous inventions and attempting to improve upon their designs. Edison's phonograph was also the first machine that was able to play back the sound it recorded. Scott's phonautograph could only record sounds; it could not play them back. Others cite Edison's lightbulb as a stolen invention because it was not the first lightbulb ever invented. However, Edison was always up front about taking inspiration and research from inventors and scientists who had gone before him. The previous inventors had gone as far as they could go with a certain invention, and Edison's plan was to improve upon it and take it even further, which he did with his lightbulb.

Another controversial invention was the first motion-picture camera. While it's true Edison had the idea for the camera, Edison himself did not actually create the kinetograph. He had a vision of creating moving pictures complete with sound, but he did not know how to make this happen. So he did what he often did, which was to sketch out his ideas and hand them over to one of his workers. William K. L. Dickson was the one who was asked by Edison to try to create his idea of a motion-picture camera. Dickson did just that, and the kinetograph was born. However, the kinetograph was patented under Edison's name, not Dickson's. Many people use the patent to argue that Edison stole Dickson's invention. However, others argue that Dickson was not an independent inventor but rather one of Edison's lab assistants. He was hired by Edison to work in his laboratory and help him with his inventions. It was a common practice then, and is still a common practice today, for scientists or companies to hire workers to assist them in creating new things. The inventions that those workers create belong to the company who hired them, not to the individual who actually created the inventions.

Edison's Failures

Behind every successful person is likely to be a series of efforts that did not work. Edison is no exception. He was made famous by his successful inventions, but he also had inventions and endeavors that were not so successful. Edison did face criticism when his ideas and investments underperformed, but he was not one to dwell on his failures.

Edison's kinetograph and kinetoscope paved the way for movies as we know them today. The first movie camera, seen here, is on display in the Thomas Edison National Historical Park in West Orange, New Jersey.

CHAPTER SIX

Edison's Lasting Legacy

Almost one hundred years after his death, Thomas Edison is still remembered for his contributions to science and technology. Many things that we have today would not exist without his work and inventions, including electricity, sources of entertainment, and many things that make everyday life more convenient. His memory is preserved today through several technology-based organizations, educational institutions, museums, parks, and awards.

Edison Immortalized

Edison was recognized and revered for his work while he was alive, and that recognition has continued long after

Edison is seen here in 1911 while visiting Washington, DC.

his death. Even in the twenty-first century, Edison continues to receive recognition for his many inventions.

In 2010, *Time* magazine did a story about Edison titled "The Making of America: Thomas Edison," in which Edison's many inventions and contributions to technology were highlighted. The story even suggested that Silicon Valley, California, today's hub of technology and innovation, is a contemporary version of Edison's Menlo Park laboratory.

Also in 2010, the Recording Academy presented a special Grammy Award to Thomas Edison for his contributions to the recording and music industry with the invention of the phonograph. The Recording Academy issued the following statement with their announcement of the award:

> In 1877, he gained public fame for his patent of the phonograph, the first device to record and reproduce sound. Edison's tabletop phonograph was integral in revolutionizing entertainment by bringing music into the homes of people all around the world.[1]

During his lifetime, Edison had ideas about potential uses for the phonograph, including recording music. The music industry as we know it today got its start thanks to Edison's invention. One can't help but wonder what Edison's reaction would be if he could see how far voice and music recording have come since he first recited a children's nursery rhyme in his Menlo Park laboratory.

National Inventors' Day

On January 12, 1983, President Ronald Reagan, the fortieth president of the United States, established a National Inventors'

A family member of Thomas Edison is seen here accepting a Grammy Award on his behalf in 2010 for his contributions to the recording and music industry.

Day to be observed annually on February 11, the anniversary of Thomas Edison's birth. In his proclamation, President Reagan cited the great contributions inventors have made and continue to make to America's progress:

> In recognition of the enormous contribution inventors make to the nation and the world, the Congress, pursuant to Senate Joint Resolution 140 (Public Law 97-198), has designated February 11, 1983, the anniversary of the birth of Thomas Alva Edison, one of America's most famous and prolific inventors, as National Inventors' Day. Such recognition is especially appropriate at a time when our country is striving to maintain its global position as a leader in innovation and technology. Key to our future success will be the dedication and creativity of inventors.[2]

Though it remains a lesser known and less-celebrated day outside of science and technology groups, National Inventors' Day is still observed each year in America on the anniversary of Thomas Edison's birthday. It is a tribute to Edison and other inventors whose examples continue to lead and inspire the students, scientists, and inventors of today.

Parks and Museums

Edison's legacy as an inventor has been preserved through many parks and museums dedicated to his life and work. The sites of many of Edison's former buildings, including his homes and laboratories, have been turned into historic sites and museums. Parks, buildings, and even streets have been named after the famed inventor, keeping his legacy alive today.

Menlo Park Museum

Menlo Park, New Jersey, was a small town made famous by an inventor so creative and productive he was nicknamed a "wizard." Menlo Park remains in the spotlight even today, over a century after Edison chose to call it home and produced his most famous inventions there. The Thomas Edison Center at Menlo Park in New Jersey is a 36-acre (14.5-hectare) state park that includes a museum dedicated to Edison's work. Visitors can view artifacts and inventions from his laboratory as well as listen to phonographs that are over one hundred years old.

Edison's Glenmont Estate and Laboratory

Menlo Park was not Edison's only residence or laboratory that has been preserved as a tribute to his work. The Thomas Edison National Historical Park in West Orange, New Jersey is the location of his final home. The park includes Glenmont Estate, the family home, as well as Edison's laboratory. It features three different collections for visitors to experience. The historical artifacts collection includes over three hundred thousand items, the archives collection includes approximately five million documents, and the natural history collection consists of plant specimens taken from Glenmont Estate.

Edison Birthplace Museum

Menlo Park and West Orange are not the only places of significance when it comes to the life of Thomas Edison. A museum dedicated to Edison has also been established in his birthplace of Milan, Ohio. The Thomas A. Edison Birthplace Museum is located in the city of Milan on North Edison Drive, a street that was named in his honor. The museum is unique from other Edison museums because Edison's wife, Mina, and

Thomas Edison's second wife, Mina, and their daughter turned Edison's birthplace in Milan, Ohio, into a museum dedicated to Edison's life and career.

their daughter, Madeleine, established it in his honor. They wanted to remind the public of Edison's humble beginnings, when his family struggled financially, and of how much he overcame and accomplished during his lifetime.

General Electric

After Edison began his work with electricity, he formed the Edison General Electric Company in 1890. However, he was not the only one working on an electrical system. The Thomson-Houston Electric Company soon emerged as a competitor. Both companies worked to deliver electricity to the public, but they each struggled in certain areas and were unable to use each other's patented devices and technologies. The solution was to merge the two companies, and in 1892, the General Electric Company was formed.

The General Electric Company still exists today, carrying on Edison's legacy of technology and innovation. For over 125 years, the General Electric Company has been delivering lighting, industrial products, power transmissions, and home appliances to the public. The General Electric Company also maintains a history museum, the Hall of Electrical History, located in Schenectady, New York, where General Electric is headquartered. The museum contains historical information about the General Electric Company and the history of electricity, as well as historical photographs documenting the early days of the company.

Today's Technology

Edison's legacy lives on today in many ways, but perhaps the most significant is the role his inventions play in everyday life

THOMAS A. EDISON PATENT AWARD

Just as in Edison's time, many people in the United States today have dedicated their educations and careers to science and technology. There are many clubs, organizations, and societies dedicated to science. One society is the American Society of Mechanical Engineers. Mechanical engineers are those who work designing, building, and improving machines. The American Society of Mechanical Engineers is a nonprofit society. Its goal is to promote mechanical engineering through education, training, and research.

One way the society encourages the advancement of science and technology is by offering an annual award called the Thomas A. Edison Patent Award. Patents are just as important for scientists and inventors today as they were in Edison's time. In today's world of science and technology and a global community connected through the internet, it is important to patent one's work to protect it from theft or from simply missing out if someone else patents the same process or invention first. The Thomas A. Edison Patent Award started in 1997 and is still given each year. The award recognizes an individual whose "creativity of a patented device or process [has] the potential of significantly enhancing some aspect of mechanical engineering."[3]

Edison's name continues to be attached to awards and honors, such as this patent award, in the fields of science, technology, and engineering as a tribute to his contributions in the fields and as a way of keeping his legacy alive.

in the twenty-first century. Many things that are used today can be attributed to Edison's work, either his own invention or his improvement upon an existing one.

Indoor Electricity

The majority of things used today run on electricity. Homes, offices, schools, libraries, and every other kind of building use electricity. They use it for lighting, for heating and cooling, for elevators, for security systems, and many more things. Edison's determination to invent a safe, affordable, incandescent lightbulb made indoor electricity common. Today, when you go to turn on a light, charge a cell phone, or use a computer, you probably don't think much about the electrical system that makes it all possible. Thanks to Edison's efforts, we can simply flip a switch and have power when we need it.

Although Edison was a pioneer in bringing safe electrical lighting indoors, it is not Edison's direct current system that is most commonly used in homes today. Ironically, Tesla's system of alternating current is used to provide electricity to homes. Alternating current is generally considered safer than Edison's direct current. This is because it can reduce the amount of electricity being sent over a connection from a dangerously high amount to a lower amount that is safe for use.

Electric Cars

Another area where Edison's legacy lives on today is with electric cars. While electric cars are becoming more and more common today, they were not common when automobiles were first introduced. Edison believed that automobiles should be battery-powered rather than gasoline-powered. He thought automobiles would be safer for the environment and last longer if they ran on rechargeable batteries. His battery-powered

Edison's lightbulb has come a long way since its creation in Menlo Park. Today, we can find multiple kinds of lightbulbs and lighting inside one building, such as in the restaurant pictured here.

automobile was never made a reality though. Once Henry Ford's gasoline-powered Model T became a sensation, Edison abandoned his efforts to make a battery strong enough to power an automobile.

While Edison did not create electric cars, his thinking was very much ahead of his time, and his vision of electric cars is being realized today. It is ironic that one of the largest manufacturers of electric cars is a company that takes its name from Edison's great rival, Tesla.

Entertainment

The motion-picture industry is a very popular form of entertainment today. Films have evolved from silent, black-and-white shorts to movies lasting hours at a time and including audio, special effects, and computer animation. Motion pictures today are used for entertainment, education, and political activism. Actors, actresses, directors, writers, technical engineers, and artists have all made careers out of the motion-picture industry. Most people going to the movies today probably don't stop to reflect on the industry and the technology that went into creating motion pictures. It might seem funny to think that it all started with Edison filming a man sneezing. But with a three-second sneeze caught on film came the birth of the industry we know and enjoy today.

Similarly to the motion-picture industry, Edison's work has had a profound impact on the music industry. When you go to listen to, stream, or download music today, you probably don't stop to reflect on what makes that possible. While technology—especially computer technology—has greatly enhanced and improved voice recordings, it's important to remember that it all started with Edison reciting a children's nursery rhyme. Recording the human voice and taking videos today is not uncommon. Most people do these things on their cell phones regularly. However, it's worth stopping and reflecting on Edison's contributions to these two forms of entertainment and how they carry his legacy forward even today.

Despite being born over a century ago, Edison's life and work are still relevant today. Many of his inventions are still in use and have been improved upon over the years, bringing advancements in technology. His perseverance has been an example for inventors of the twentieth and twenty-first centuries. He was forward-thinking, envisioning things that did not yet exist, and working to make them a reality. His curiosity, innovative thinking, and desire to be the best made him one of the most successful, most controversial, and most well-remembered entrepreneurs of all time.

CHRONOLOGY

1790 The Patent Act is passed and signed by President George Washington.

1844 The first telegraph message is transmitted.

1847 Thomas Alva Edison is born in Milan, Ohio.

1859 Edison takes his first job working for the railroad.

1861 The Civil War begins with a violent battle at Fort Sumter, South Carolina.

1862 Edison begins learning professional telegraphy.

1865 The Civil War ends, and the Thirteenth Amendment to the US Constitution is ratified.

1869 Edison receives his first patent for an electric vote-counting machine and pursues inventing full time.

1871 Edison marries Mary Stilwell.

1873 Daughter Marion is born.

1874 Edison invents and sells his telegraph invention, the quadruplex.

1876 Edison moves his laboratory to Menlo Park, New Jersey. Son Thomas Alva Edison Jr. is born.

1876 Alexander Graham Bell patents the telephone, and the first telephone call is made.

1877 Edison invents the phonograph.

1878 Son William is born.

1879 Edison gives the first public demonstration of his new incandescent lightbulb.

1882 Edison illuminates 1 square mile (2.5 square kilometers) of downtown Manhattan in New York City.

1884 Edison's wife, Mary, dies after an extended illness.

1884 Nikola Tesla immigrates to America and begins working for Edison.

1885 Tesla quits working for Edison over a payment dispute.

1886 Edison gets married for the second time, to Mina Miller.

1888 Daughter Madeleine is born.

1890 Son Charles is born.

1892 The General Electric Company forms as the result of merging Edison General Electric Company and the Thomson-Houston Electric Company.

1896 Edison meets Henry Ford and the two form a lasting friendship.

1896 Nikola Tesla's hydroelectric power plant is used to power the city of Buffalo, New York.

1897 Edison patents the first motion-picture camera, the kinetograph.

1898 Son Theodore is born.

1914 An explosion occurs in Edison's concrete lab in West Orange, New Jersey.

1925 Edison pens the essay "The Philosophy of Thomas Paine."

1931 Edison dies at age eighty-four at his Glenmont Estate in New Jersey.

GLOSSARY

abolitionist A person working to end slavery.

Age of Reform A period in America from 1830 to 1850 in which many people were calling for social changes.

alternating current A flow of electricity that moves forward and backward and can change the amount of electricity being sent to different places.

arc lighting An early form of electrical lighting in which an electric arc forms between two carbon rods.

artisan Someone who crafts goods by hand from start to finish.

assembly line A form of manufacturing where machines and people work one by one to build projects like automobiles. Each worker has a different task for which they are responsible.

Civil War Fought from 1861 to 1865, this conflict divided the United States between north and south after seven slave states seceded from the rest of the country.

direct current A flow of electricity in one direction that maintains the same amount of power at all times.

entrepreneur A person who starts his or her own business.

gold rush A period of mining for gold in California that began in 1848 and continued for almost ten years.

hydroelectric Using the power of rushing water to create electricity.

immigration When one leaves his or her home country to live in another country.

incandescent Creating light through heat.

industrialization When a large amount of machine-powered factories are concentrated in one area.

Industrial Revolution A period in Great Britain and America from the late 1700s to the early 1900s when machines and factories began replacing manual labor, farmers, and artisans.

innovation A new and unique approach to a task, idea, or product.

kinetograph A device capable of recording motion that was used to film the first patented motion picture.

kinetoscope A device with a viewing hole through which one could view motion pictures filmed with a kinetograph.

Louisiana Purchase When America doubled its size by purchasing the Louisiana Territory from France in 1803.

mechanization When machines do work that has traditionally been done by hand.

Mexican-American War A war fought between the United States and Mexico from 1846 to 1848 over the Texas border and how much territory America could claim.

Morse Code A communications system developed in 1835 by Samuel Morse in which numbers and letters were replaced with dots and dashes.

patent An official document granting someone the rights to an invention and prohibiting others from making it without the inventor's permission.

Patent Act A law passed by the US Congress on April 10, 1790, allowing citizens to protect their inventions and creative works with a patent.

phonograph A device that could record and play back sound.

pull factors Events or consequences that make someone want to immigrate to another country, such as the hope of freedom and economic opportunity.

push factors Events or consequences that force someone to leave their home country for another, such as poverty and government oppression.

revolutionize To dramatically transform something, often improving a process or making something more productive.

secede To officially leave something, such as individual states that officially left the United States during the Civil War.

Spanish-American War A brief war between the United States and Spain, fought in 1898, over Spain's control of Cuba. It was the first war to have footage captured on film by a motion-picture camera.

telegraph A fast way of sending messages using electric devices and Morse Code that revolutionized communication in the nineteenth century.

temperance Refraining from alcoholic beverages.

Thirteenth Amendment An amendment to the US Constitution made official in 1865 that made slavery illegal.

Transcontinental Railroad The first railroad to cross the entire United States and connect the Pacific and Atlantic coasts.

urbanization The development of cities and increased population around factories.

War of the Currents A feud between George Westinghouse, Nikola Tesla, and Thomas Edison for control over the electricity market.

women's suffrage A movement to win women the right to vote.

SOURCES

CHAPTER ONE

1. Clare D. McGillem, "Telegraph," *Encyclopedia Britannica*, December 7, 2016, https://www.britannica.com/technology/telegraph.

2. Mark C. Carnes and John A. Garraty, *American Destiny Narrative of a Nation Volume I to 1877* (New York: Pearson Longman, 2006), 318.

3. "Nineteenth Amendment to the US Constitution: Women's Right to Vote (1920)," Our Documents, Accessed August 16, 2018, https://www.ourdocuments.gov/doc.php?flash=false&doc=63.

4. "Thirteenth Amendment to the US Constitution: Abolition of Slavery (1865)," Our Documents, Accessed August 16, 2018, https://www.ourdocuments.gov/doc.php?flash=false&doc=40.

CHAPTER TWO

1. Jan Adkins, *Thomas Edison: A Photographic Story of a Life* (New York: DK Publishing, 2009), 17.

2. Ibid., 19.

3. "Thomas Edison on Failure," Edison Muckers, Accessed August 30, 2018, http://www.edisonmuckers.org/thomas-edison-on-failure.

4. Ibid.

5. Adkins, *Thomas Edison: A Photographic Story of a Life* (New York: DK Publishing, 2009), 70.

CHAPTER THREE

1. David Hochfelder, "Alexander Graham Bell," Encyclopedia Britannica, August 3, 2017, https://www.britannica.com/biography/Alexander-Graham-Bell.

2. Ibid.3. "The U.S. Patent System Celebrates 212 Years," United States Patent and Trademark Office, April 9, 2002, https://www.uspto.gov/about-us/news-updates/us-patent-system-celebrates-212-years.

4. Nigel Cawthorne, *Tesla vs. Edison: The Life-Long Feud that Electrified the World (*New York: Chartwell, 2016), 13.

CHAPTER FOUR

1. "History of the Cylinder Phonograph," Library of Congress, Accessed August 26, 2018, https://www.loc.gov/collections/edison-company-motion-pictures-and-sound-recordings/articles-and-essays/history-of-edison-sound-recordings/history-of-the-cylinder-phonograph.

2. Ibid.

3. Jan Adkins, *Thomas Edison: A Photographic Story of a Life* (New York: DK Publishing, 2009), 98.

4. Ibid., 77.

5. "History of Edison Motion Pictures," Library of Congress, Accessed August 27, 2018, https://www.loc.gov/collections/ edison-company-motion-pictures-and-sound-recordings/ articles-and-essays/history-of-edison-motion-pictures.

CHAPTER FIVE

1. Theresa M. Collins and Lisa Gitelman, *Thomas Edison and Modern America: A Brief History with Documents* (New York: Palgrave, 2002), 86.

2. Thomas Alva Edison, "The Philosophy of Thomas Paine by Thomas Edison," Thomas Paine National Historical Association, June 7, 1925, http://thomaspaine.org/ aboutpaine/the-philosophy-of-thomas-paine-by-thomas-edison.html.

3. Theresa M. Collins and Lisa Gitelman, *Thomas Edison and Modern America: A Brief History with Documents* (New York: Palgrave, 2002), 67.

4. Randall Stross, *The Wizard of Menlo Park: How Thomas Alva Edison Invented the Modern World* (New York: Crown, 2007), 191.

CHAPTER SIX

1. Richard Payerchin, "Edison to Receive Grammy for Phonograph," The Morning Journal News, December 15, 2009, www.morningjournal.com/article/MJ/20091215/NEWS/312159970.

2. Ronald Reagan, "Proclamation 5013 – National Inventors' Day, 1983," The American Presidency Project, January 12, 1983, http://www.presidency.ucsb.edu/ws/index.php?pid=41232.

3. "Thomas A. Edison Patent Award," The American Society of Mechanical Engineers, Accessed September 1, 2018, https://www.asme.org/about-asme/participate/honors-awards/achievement-awards/thomas-a-edison-patent-award.

FURTHER INFORMATION

BOOKS

Cawthorne, Nigel. *Tesla vs. Edison: The Life-Long Feud That Electrified the World.* New York: Chartwell, 2016.

Colman, Penny. *Elizabeth Cady Stanton and Susan B. Anthony: A Friendship That Changed the World.* New York: Square Fish, 2016.

Douglass, Frederick. *A Narrative of the Life of Frederick Douglass.* Ottawa, Canada: East India Publishing Company, 2018.

Kendrick, Kathleen M., and Peter Liebhold. *Smithsonian Treasures of American History.* Washington, DC: Smithsonian Books, 2016.

Kennedy, Alexander. *Thomas Edison: Inventing the Modern World.* New York: Fritzen, 2017.

WEBSITES

General Electric YouTube Channel
https://www.youtube.com/ge

The General Electric Company, formed over one hundred years ago, still exists today. GE has their own YouTube channel where students can explore a variety of videos about the ways GE is working to bring innovation and technology to the world through new inventions.

Library of Congress
https://www.loc.gov

Students can use this website to search for many topics in American History. They may learn more about Thomas Edison and his inventions, the Industrial Revolution, the Civil War, and many more famous Americans and events that shaped our country.

United States Patent and Trademark Office
https://www.uspto.gov/kids/teens.html

This is a page on the US Patent and Trademark Office website dedicated to educating teens about patents. Students can learn about teen inventors who have received patents, watch educational videos, and view answers to common questions about patents, trademarks, and copyrights.

MUSEUMS

Edison and Ford Winter Estates
2350 McGregor Blvd.
Fort Myers, FL 33901

Smithsonian National Museum of American History
The National Mall at Constitution Avenue NW
Washington, DC

Thomas A. Edison Birthplace Museum
9 N Edison Dr.
Milan, OH 44846

Thomas Edison Center at Menlo Park
37 Christie St.
Edison, NJ 08820

Thomas Edison National Historical Park
211 Main Street
West Orange, NJ 07052

BIBLIOGRAPHY

"About Scientific American." *Scientific American.* Accessed August 28, 2018. https://www.scientificamerican.com/page/about-scientific-american.

Adkins, Jan. *Thomas Edison: A Photographic Story of a Life.* New York: DK Publishing, 2009.

"An Age of Reform." *Encyclopedia Britannica.* Accessed August 10, 2018. https://www.britannica.com19/place/United-States/An-age-of-reform.

"Alexander Graham Bell." History. Last modified August 21, 2018. https://www.history.com/topics/inventions/alexander-graham-bell.

"American Newspapers, 1800–1860: An Introduction." University of Illinois at Urbana Champaign. https://www.library.illinois.edu/hpnl/tutorials/antebellum-newspapers-introduction.

"The Beginnings of American Railroads and Mapping." Library of Congress. Accessed August 14, 2018. https://www.loc.gov/collections/railroad-maps-1828-to-1900/articles-and-essays/history-of-railroads-and-maps/the-beginnings-of-american-railroads-and-mapping.

Carnes, Mark C., and John A. Garraty. *American Destiny Narrative of a Nation Volume I (to 1877).* New York: Pearson Longman, 2006.

Cawthorne, Nigel. *Tesla vs. Edison The Life-Long Feud That Electrified the World.* New York: Chartwell, 2016.

Collins, Theresa M., and Lisa Gitelman. *Thomas Edison and Modern America: A Brief History with Documents.* New York: Palgrave, 2002.

Cremin, Lawrence A. "Horace Mann: American Educator." *Encyclopedia Britannica.* Last modified July 29, 2018. https://www.britannica.com/biography/Horace-Mann.

DuMont, Brianna. *Thrilling Thieves, Liars, Cheats, and Cons Who Changed History.* New York: Sky Pony, 2018.

Edison, Thomas. "The Philosophy of Thomas Paine by Thomas Edison." Thomas Paine National Historical Association. Accessed August 16, 2018. http://thomaspaine.org/aboutpaine/the-philosophy-of-thomas-paine-by-thomas-edison.html.

"Edison and Ford: A Lasting Friendship." The Henry Ford. Accessed August 28, 2018. https://www.thehenryford.org/collections-and-research/digital-collections/expert-sets/101111.

"Edison's Patents." Rutgers School of Arts and Sciences. http://edison.rutgers.edu/patents.htm.

Gelderman, Carol W. "Henry Ford: American Industrialist." *Encyclopedia Britannica.* Last modified July 26, 2018. https://www.britannica.com/biography/Henry-Ford.

"George Westinghouse: American Inventor and Industrialist." *Encyclopedia Britannica.* Last modified March 5, 2018.

https://www.britannica.com/biography/George-Westinghouse.

"Gold Discovered in California." America's Library. Accessed August 28, 2018. http://www.americaslibrary.gov/jb/reform/jb_reform_fortyniners_3.html.

"History of the Cylinder Phonograph." Library of Congress. Accessed August 11, 2018. https://www.loc.gov/collections/edison-company-motion-pictures-and-sound-recordings/articles-and-essays/history-of-edison-sound-recordings/history-of-the-cylinder-phonograph.

Hochfelder, David. "Alexander Graham Bell: American Inventor." *Encyclopedia Britannica*. Last modified August 3, 2018. https://www.britannica.com/biography/Alexander-Graham-Bell.

"Home." Thomas A. Edison Birthplace Museum. Accessed August 13, 2018. http://tomedison.org.

"Incandescent Lamp." *Encyclopedia Britannica*. Last modified August 4, 2016. https://www.britannica.com/technology/incandescent-lamp.

"The Making of America: Thomas Edison." *Time*. Accessed August 21, 2018. http://content.time.com/time/specials/packages/0,28757,1999143,00.html.

"The Market Revolution Impact and Significance." Khan Academy. Accessed August 28, 2018. https://www.khanacademy.org/humanities/us-history/the-early-republic/politics-society-early-19th-c/v/the-market-revolution-part-3.

McGillem, Clare D. "Telegraph." *Encyclopedia Britannica*. Last modified December 7, 2016. https://www.britannica.com/technology/telegraph.

"Mexican-American War." *Encyclopedia Britannica*. Last modified July 21, 2017. https://www.britannica.com/event/Mexican-American-War#accordion-article-history.

"Nikola Tesla Biography." Biography. Last modified April 11, 2018. https://www.biography.com/people/nikola-tesla-9504443.

"Origins of Sound Recording." National Park Service. Accessed August 15, 2018. https://www.nps.gov/edis/learn/historyculture/origins-of-sound-recording.htm.

"Origins of Sound Recording: The Inventors." National Park Service. https://www.nps.gov/edis/learn/historyculture/origins-of-sound-recording-edouard-leon-scott-de-martinville.htm.

Payerchin, Richard. "Edison to Receive Grammy for Phonograph." *Morning Journal News*. Last modified December 15, 2009. http://www.morningjournal.com/article/MJ/20091215/NEWS/312159970.

Reagan, Ronald. "Proclamation 5013 – National Inventors' Day, 1983." The American Presidency Project. http://www.presidency.ucsb.edu/ws/index.php?pid=41232.

"The Spanish-American War in Motion Pictures." Library of Congress. Accessed August 28, 2018. https://www.loc.gov/collections/spanish-american-war-in-motion-pictures/about-this-collection.

Stross, Randall. *The Wizard of Menlo Park*. New York: Crown, 2007.

"Thomas A. Edison Patent Award." The American Society of Mechanical Engineers. Accessed August 21, 2018. https://www.asme.org/about-asme/participate/honors-awards/achievement-awards/thomas-a-edison-patent-award.

"Thomas Edison & The History of Electricity." General Electric. Accessed August 9, 2018. https://www.ge.com/about-us/history/thomas-edison.

"Thomas Paine Biography." Biography. Last modified March 8, 2018. https://www.biography.com/people/thomas-paine-9431951.

"The U.S. Patent System Celebrates 212 Years." United States Patent and Trademark Office. Last modified April 9, 2002. https://www.uspto.gov/about-us/news-updates/us-patent-system-celebrates-212-years.

"Welcome to Menlo Park." The Thomas Edison Center at Menlo Park. Accessed August 9, 2018. http://www.menloparkmuseum.org.

"Where Modern America Was Invented." Thomas Edison National Historical Park. Accessed August 10, 2018. https://www.nps.gov/edis/index.htm.

"The World of 1898: The Spanish-American War." Library of Congress. Accessed August 14, 2018. http://www.loc.gov/rr/hispanic/1898/intro.html.

INDEX

Page numbers in **boldface** refer to images.

ABOUT THE AUTHOR

Kaitlin Scirri is a writer and editor of books for children, teens, and adults. She holds a bachelor's degree in writing from the State University of New York at Buffalo State. Other books by Scirri include *Civic Values: Property Rights*, *The Science of Superpowers: Invisibility and X-Ray Vision*, and *The Science of Superpowers: Controlling Electricity and Weather*. Scirri has a love of reading and history and enjoys sharing that passion with others through her writing.